Anthony Thomas Bumbales

Anthony Thomas Gumbales

School Days is a special journal for recording the highlights and memorable events of your child's school-age years, from preschool through high school. It's a scrapbook for homework and drawings, a place to keep everything from report cards to medical records, to souvenirs. And it's a photo album! Fill it with school pictures, photos of birthday parties, family members, and favorite pets.

School Days picks up where a baby book leaves off. It's a place to record your thoughts and feelings about the unique person your child is developing into. Fill in the pages as you watch your child grow and change, and over the years you will create a loving and very personal gift to present to your son or daughter upon graduation.

SCHOOL DAYS

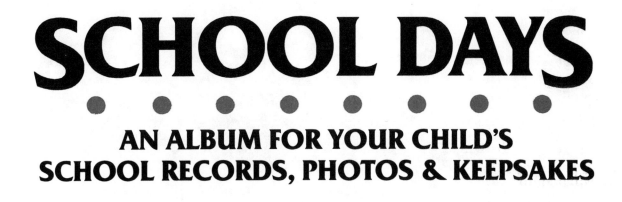

AN ALBUM FOR YOUR CHILD'S
SCHOOL RECORDS, PHOTOS & KEEPSAKES

Illustrated by Deborah Michel

Troll Associates

Contents

Our Family

Family Tree

Maternal Great-Grandparents

_____
_____
_____
_____

Paternal Great-Grandparents

_____
_____
_____
_____

Maternal Grandparents

_____
_____

Paternal Grandparents

_____
_____

Mother _____

Father _____

Brothers and Sisters

_____
_____
_____
_____

Child's Name

Aunts & Uncles

_____
_____
_____
_____
_____

Cousins

_____
_____
_____
_____
_____

Child's Album

_____

Name

_____

Birthdate

At Birth

Attach Photo Here

At One Year

Attach Photo Here

At Two Years

Attach Photo Here

At Three Years

Attach Photo Here

A Family Album

Attach Photo Here

Name _____

Date _____

Attach Photo Here

Name _____

Date _____

Attach Photo Here

Name _____

Date _____

Attach Photo Here

Name _____

Date _____

Attach Photo Here

Attach Photo Here

Name _____

Date _____

Name _____

Date _____

Godparents or
Very Special Family Friends

Attach Photo Here

Attach Photo Here

Name _____

Date _____

Name _____

Date _____

PRESCHOOL

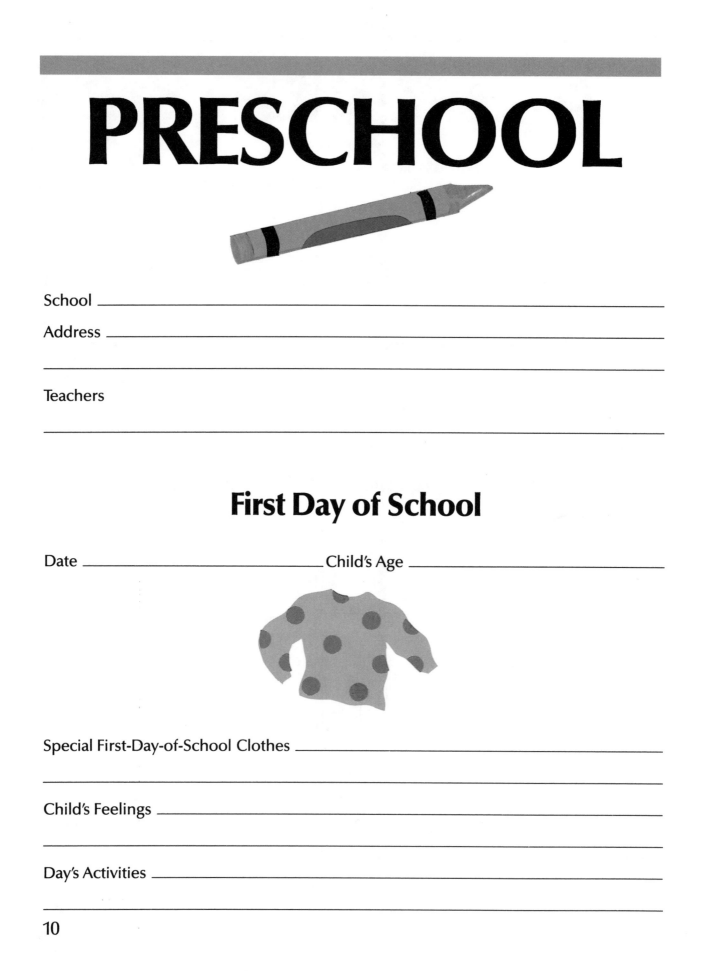

School _____

Address _____

_____

Teachers _____

_____

First Day of School

Date _____ Child's Age _____

Special First-Day-of-School Clothes _____

_____

Child's Feelings _____

_____

Day's Activities _____

_____

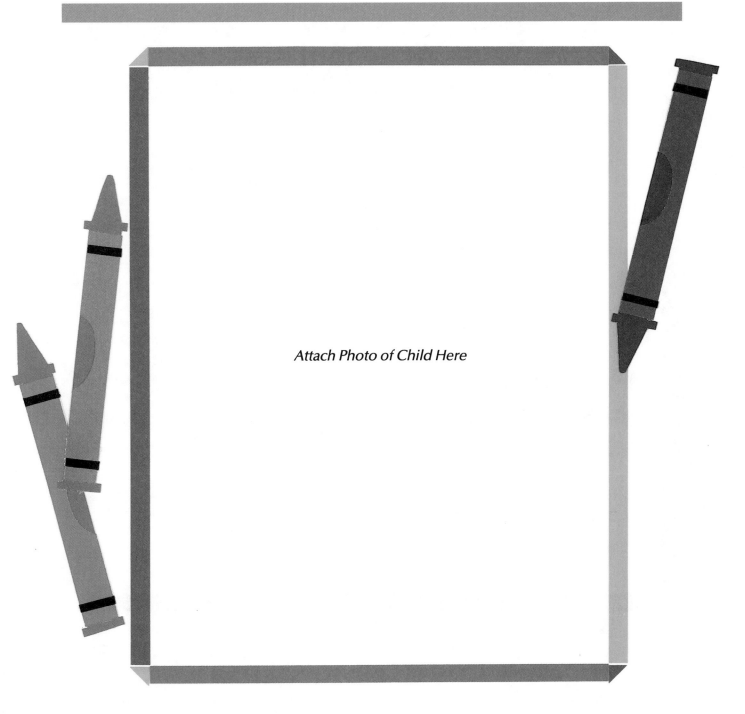

Attach Photo of Child Here

My Reflections on This Day _____

_____

_____

_____

At School

*Attach Class Photo or
Pictures of Classmates Here*

Classmates

_____	_____
_____	_____
_____	_____
_____	_____
_____	_____
_____	_____

Activities _____

_____

Toys _____

_____

Songs _____

_____

Classroom Pets _____

Special Projects _____

_____

Important Accomplishments _____

_____

_____

Attach Sample of Schoolwork Here

Feelings About School _____

_____

_____

Special Events at School

Class Trip

A Visit to _____ Date _____

Details _____

_____

Visitor to School

Name _____ Date _____

Details _____

_____

Special School Days and Holiday Celebrations

Occasion _____ Date _____

Details _____

_____

Occasion _____ Date _____

Details _____

Keepsakes

Attach Pocket Here
(See back of book for instructions)

Happy Birthday!

Age _____ Celebration Date _____

Place _____

Special Visitors and Guests _____

_____

_____

_____

Gifts _____

_____

_____

Games and Activities _____

_____

Highlights _____

_____

_____

*Attach Party Invitation
or Birthday Photo Here*

Favorites

Playmates _____

_____

Games _____

Books _____

_____

Songs _____

Television Shows _____

Toys _____

Stuffed Animals _____

Clothes _____

Foods _____

Places to Go _____

Things to Do _____

_____

At Home

*Attach Photo
of Home Here*

Address _____

_____

Favorite Family Activities _____

_____

Family Pets _____

*Attach Photo
of Family Members or Pets Here*

Vacations and Visits

A Trip to _____ Date _____

Details _____

_____

_____

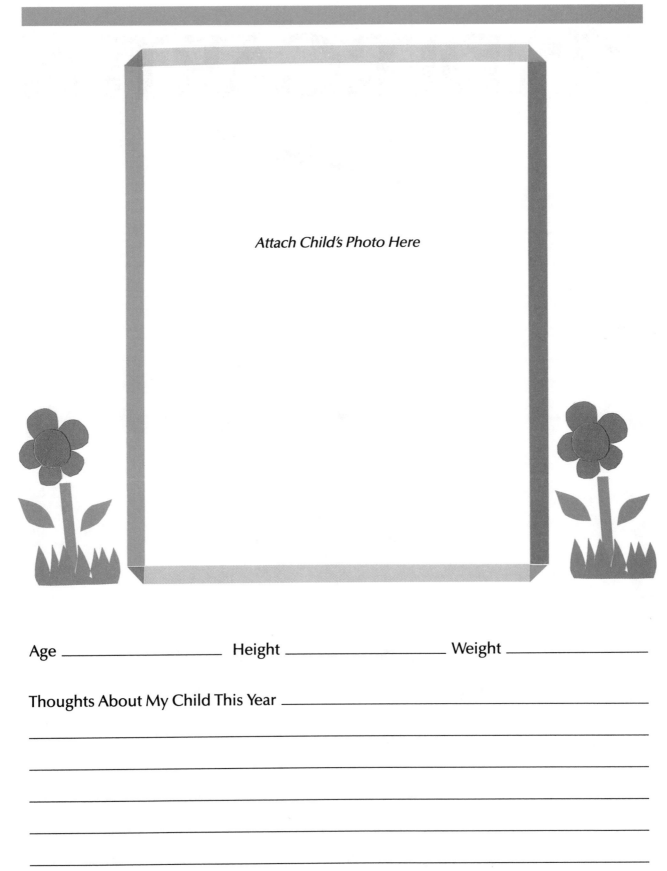

Attach Child's Photo Here

Age _____ Height _____ Weight _____

Thoughts About My Child This Year _____

_____

_____

_____

_____

_____

KINDERGARTEN

School _____

Address _____

_____

Teachers

_____   _____

*Attach Class Photo or
Pictures of Classmates Here*

Classmates

_____   _____

_____   _____

_____   _____

_____   _____

At School

Activities _____

_____

Toys _____

_____

Songs _____

_____

Classroom Pets _____

Special Projects _____

_____

Important Accomplishments _____

_____

_____

Attach Sample of Schoolwork Here

Feelings About School _____

_____

Special Events at School

Class Trip

A Visit to _____ Date _____

Details _____

_____

Visitor to School

Name _____ Date _____

Details _____

_____

Special School Days and Holiday Celebrations

Occasion _____ Date _____

Details _____

_____

Occasion _____ Date _____

Details _____

Keepsakes

Attach Pocket Here
(See back of book for instructions)

Happy Birthday!

Age _____ Celebration Date _____

Place _____

Special Visitors and Guests _____

_____

_____

_____

Gifts _____

_____

_____

Games and Activities _____

_____

Highlights _____

_____

_____

*Attach Party Invitation
or Birthday Photo Here*

Favorites

Playmates _____

_____

Games _____

Books _____

_____

Songs _____

Television Shows _____

Toys _____

Stuffed Animals _____

Clothes _____

Foods _____

Places to Go _____

Things to Do _____

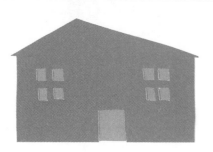

At Home

*Attach Photo
of Home Here*

Address _____

_____

Favorite Family Activities _____

_____

Family Pets _____

*Attach Photo
of Family Members or Pets Here*

Vacations and Visits

A Trip to _____ Date _____

Details _____

_____

_____

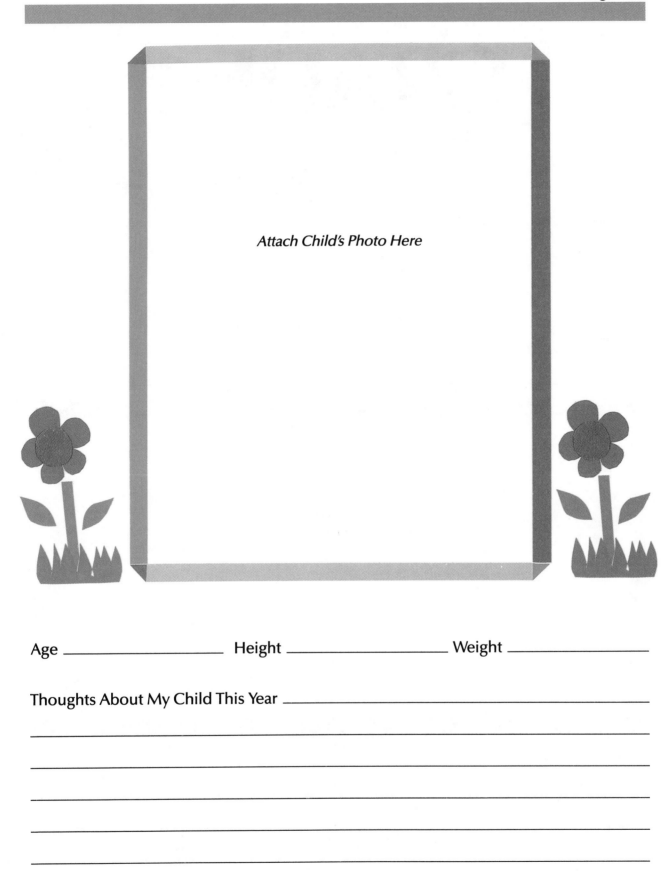

Attach Child's Photo Here

Age _____ Height _____ Weight _____

Thoughts About My Child This Year _____

_____

_____

_____

_____

_____

GRADE 1

School _____

Address _____

Teachers

_____   _____

_____   _____

*Attach Class Photo
or Pictures of Classmates Here*

Classmates

_____   _____

_____   _____

_____   _____

28

At School

Most Favorite Subject _____

Least Favorite Subject _____

Fun Activities at School _____

_____

Classroom Pets _____

Special Projects _____

_____

Important Accomplishments _____

_____

_____

After-School Activities _____

_____

Attach Sample of Schoolwork Here

Feelings About School _____

_____

_____

Special Events

Class Trips

A Visit to _____ Date _____

Details _____

_____

A Visit to _____ Date _____

Details _____

_____

Visitors to School

Name _____ Date _____

Details _____

_____

Name _____ Date _____

Details _____

_____

Special School Days and Holiday Celebrations

Occasion _____ Date _____

Details _____

_____

Occasion _____ Date _____

Details _____

_____

Sample Schoolwork, Report Cards, Keepsakes

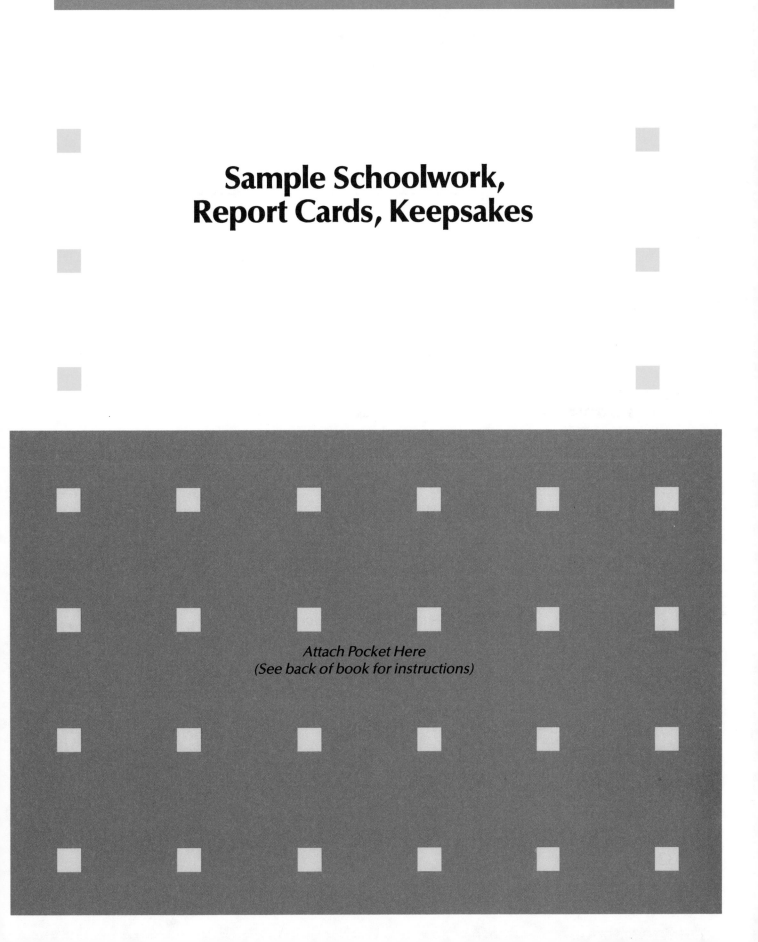

Attach Pocket Here
(See back of book for instructions)

Happy Birthday!

Age _____ Celebration Date _____

Place _____

Special Visitors and Guests _____

_____

_____

_____

Gifts _____

_____

_____

_____

Games and Activities _____

_____

Highlights _____

_____

_____

*Attach Party Invitation
or Birthday Photo Here*

Favorites

Playmates _____

_____

Games _____

_____

Books _____

_____

Songs _____

_____

Television Shows _____

Toys _____

Stuffed Animals _____

Clothes _____

Foods _____

Places to Go _____

Things to Do _____

_____

_____

At Home

Address _____

_____

Favorite Family Activities _____

_____

Family Pets _____

*Attach Photo of Family Members
or Pets Here*

Vacations and Visits

A Trip to _____ Date _____

Details _____

_____

_____

A Trip to _____ Date _____

Details _____

_____

Attach Child's Photo Here

Age _____ Height _____ Weight _____

Child's Signature _____

Thoughts About My Child This Year _____

_____

_____

_____

_____

_____

GRADE 2

School _____

Address _____

Teachers

_____ _____

_____ _____

*Attach Class Photo
or Pictures of Classmates Here*

Classmates

_____ _____

_____ _____

_____ _____

At School

Most Favorite Subject _____

Least Favorite Subject _____

Fun Activities at School _____

_____

Classroom Pets _____

Special Projects _____

_____

Important Accomplishments _____

_____

_____

After-School Activities _____

_____

Attach Sample of Schoolwork Here

Feelings About School _____

_____

_____

Special Events

Class Trips

A Visit to _____ Date _____

Details _____

_____

A Visit to _____ Date _____

Details _____

_____

Visitors to School

Name _____ Date _____

Details _____

_____

Name _____ Date _____

Details _____

_____

Special School Days and Holiday Celebrations

Occasion _____ Date _____

Details _____

_____

Occasion _____ Date _____

Details _____

_____

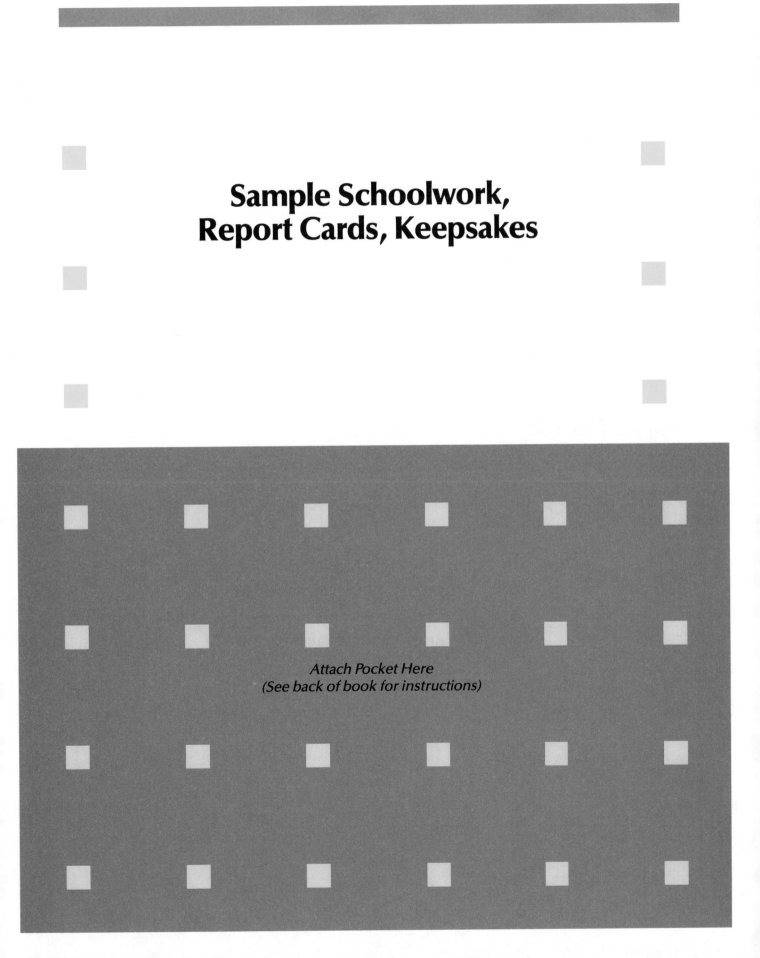

Sample Schoolwork,
Report Cards, Keepsakes

Attach Pocket Here
(See back of book for instructions)

Happy Birthday!

Age _____ Celebration Date _____

Place _____

Special Visitors and Guests _____

_____

_____

_____

Gifts _____

_____

_____

_____

Games and Activities _____

_____

Highlights _____

_____

_____

*Attach Party Invitation
or Birthday Photo Here*

Favorites

Playmates _____

_____

Games _____

_____

Books _____

_____

Songs _____

_____

Television Shows _____

Toys _____

Stuffed Animals _____

Clothes _____

Foods _____

Places to Go _____

Things to Do _____

_____

At Home

Address _____

_____

Favorite Family Activities _____

_____

Family Pets _____

*Attach Photo of Family Members
or Pets Here*

Vacations and Visits

A Trip to _____ Date _____

Details _____

_____

_____

A Trip to _____ Date _____

Details _____

_____

_____

Attach Child's Photo Here

Age _____ Height _____ Weight _____

Child's Signature _____

Thoughts About My Child This Year _____

_____

_____

_____

_____

_____

GRADE 3

School _____

Address _____

Teachers _____ _____

_____ _____

_____ _____

*Attach Class Photo
or Pictures of Classmates Here*

Classmates

_____ _____

_____ _____

_____ _____

_____ _____

At School

Most Favorite Subject _____

Least Favorite Subject _____

Favorite Teacher _____

Special Projects _____

_____

Important Accomplishments _____

_____

_____

After-School Activities _____

_____

_____

Special Talents _____

_____

Hobbies and Interests _____

_____

Feelings About School _____

_____

_____

_____

Special Events

Class Trips

A Visit to _____ Date _____

Details _____

_____

A Visit to _____ Date _____

Details _____

_____

Visitors to School

Name _____ Date _____

Details _____

_____

Name _____ Date _____

Details _____

_____

Special School Days and Holiday Celebrations

Occasion _____ Date _____

Details _____

_____

Occasion _____ Date _____

Details _____

_____

Sample Schoolwork,
Report Cards, Keepsakes

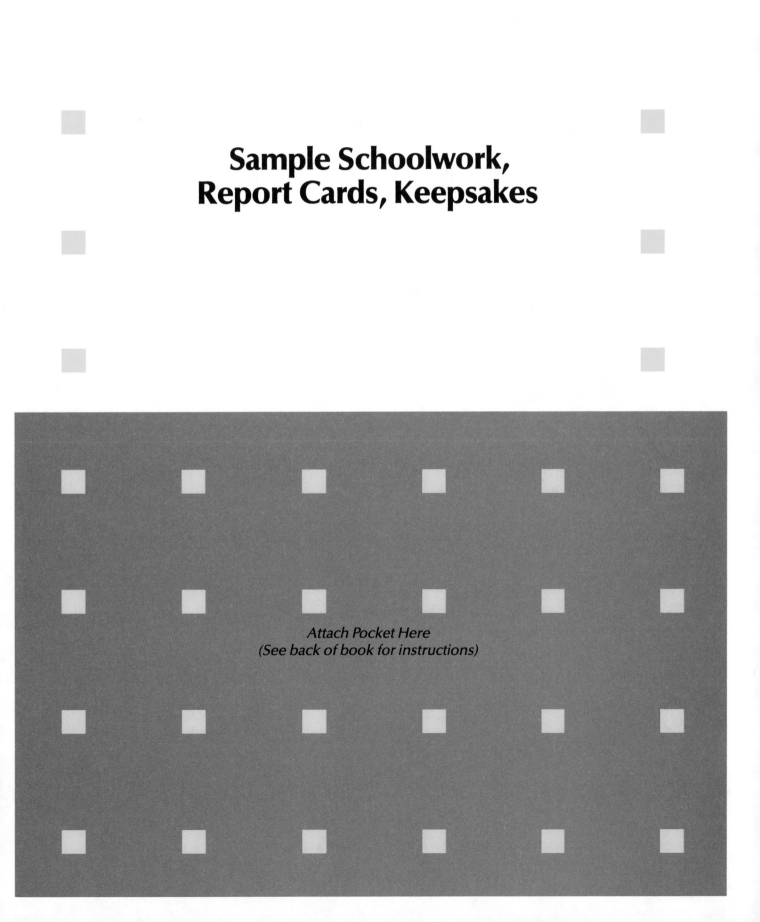

Attach Pocket Here
(See back of book for instructions)

Happy Birthday!

Age _____ Celebration Date _____

Place _____

Special Visitors and Guests _____

_____

_____

_____

Gifts _____

_____

_____

_____

Games and Activities _____

_____

Highlights _____

_____

_____

Attach Party Invitation
or Birthday Photo Here

Favorites

Friends _____
_____

Games _____

Books _____
_____

Music _____

Television Shows _____

Movies and Videos _____

Toys _____

Sports _____
_____

Clothes _____

Foods _____

Places to Go _____
_____

Things to Do _____
_____
_____

At Home

Address _____

_____

Favorite Family Activities _____

_____

_____

_____

Family Pets _____

Vacations and Visits

A Trip to _____ Date _____

Details _____

_____

A Trip to _____ Date _____

Details _____

_____

_____

Attach Souvenir
or Vacation Photo Here

Attach Child's Photo Here

Age _____ Height _____ Weight _____

Child's Signature _____

Thoughts About My Child This Year _____

_____

_____

_____

_____

_____

GRADE 4

School _____

Address _____

Teachers _____   _____

_____   _____

_____   _____

*Attach Class Photo
or Pictures of Classmates Here*

Classmates

_____   _____

_____   _____

_____   _____

_____   _____

At School

Most Favorite Subject _____

Least Favorite Subject _____

Favorite Teacher _____

Special Projects _____

_____

Important Accomplishments _____

_____

_____

After-School Activities _____

_____

_____

Special Talents _____

_____

Hobbies and Interests _____

_____

Feelings About School _____

_____

_____

_____

Special Events

Class Trips

A Visit to _____ Date _____

Details _____

_____

A Visit to _____ Date _____

Details _____

_____

Visitors to School

Name _____ Date _____

Details _____

_____

Name _____ Date _____

Details _____

_____

Special School Days and Holiday Celebrations

Occasion _____ Date _____

Details _____

_____

Occasion _____ Date _____

Details _____

_____

Sample Schoolwork,
Report Cards, Keepsakes

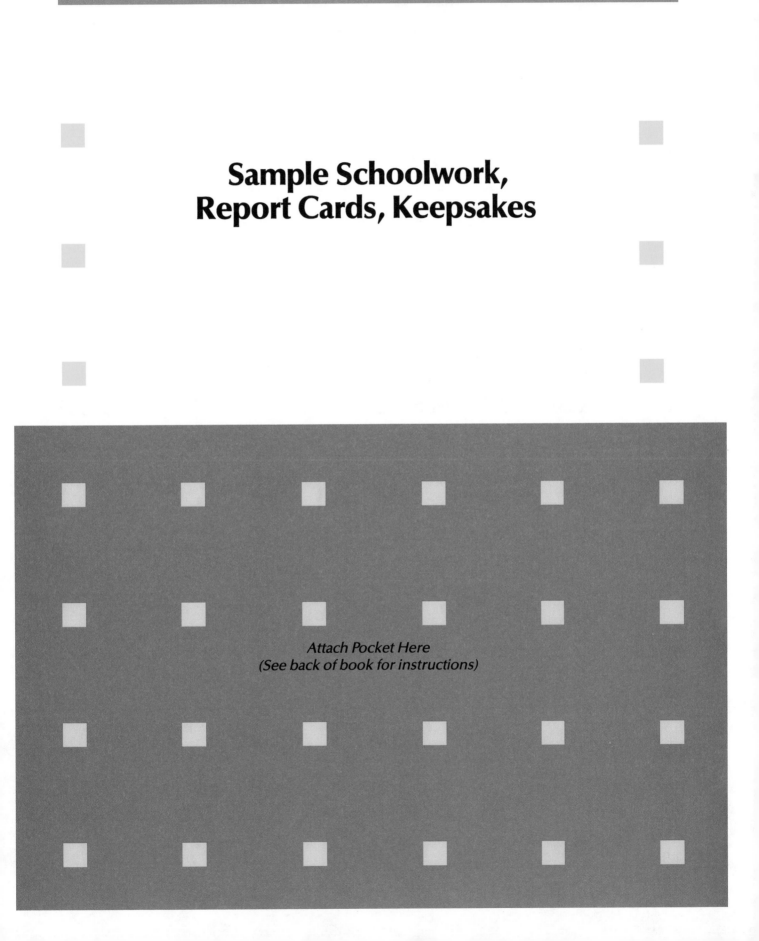

Attach Pocket Here
(See back of book for instructions)

Happy Birthday!

Age _____ Celebration Date _____

Place _____

Special Visitors and Guests _____

_____

_____

_____

Gifts _____

_____

_____

_____

Games and Activities _____

_____

Highlights _____

_____

_____

Attach Party Invitation
or Birthday Photo Here

Favorites

Friends _____

_____

Games _____

Books _____

_____

Music _____

Television Shows _____

Movies and Videos _____

Toys _____

Sports _____

_____

Clothes _____

Foods _____

Places to Go _____

_____

Things to Do _____

_____

At Home

Address _____

_____

Favorite Family Activities _____

_____

_____

_____

Family Pets _____

Vacations and Visits

A Trip to _____ Date _____

Details _____

_____

A Trip to _____ Date _____

Details _____

_____

_____

*Attach Souvenir
or Vacation Photo Here*

Attach Child's Photo Here

Age _____ Height _____ Weight _____

Child's Signature _____

Thoughts About My Child This Year _____

_____

_____

_____

_____

_____

GRADE 5

School _____

Address _____

Teachers _____   _____

_____   _____

_____   _____

Attach Class Photo
or Pictures of Classmates Here

Classmates

_____   _____

_____   _____

_____   _____

_____   _____

_____   _____

_____   _____

_____   _____

Most Favorite Subject _____

Least Favorite Subject _____

Favorite Teacher _____

Other Influential People _____

_____

Greatest Accomplishment This School Year _____

_____

School Activities and Projects _____

_____

_____

Special Talents _____

_____

Hobbies and Interests _____

_____

_____

Aspirations and Goals _____

_____

Highlights of the Year

Trip to _____ Date _____

Details _____

_____

Party for _____ Date _____

Details _____

_____

_____

_____

Special Event _____ Date _____

Details _____

_____

*Attach Photos
or Souvenirs Here*

Summer Activities _____

_____

_____

Sample Schoolwork,
Report Cards, Keepsakes

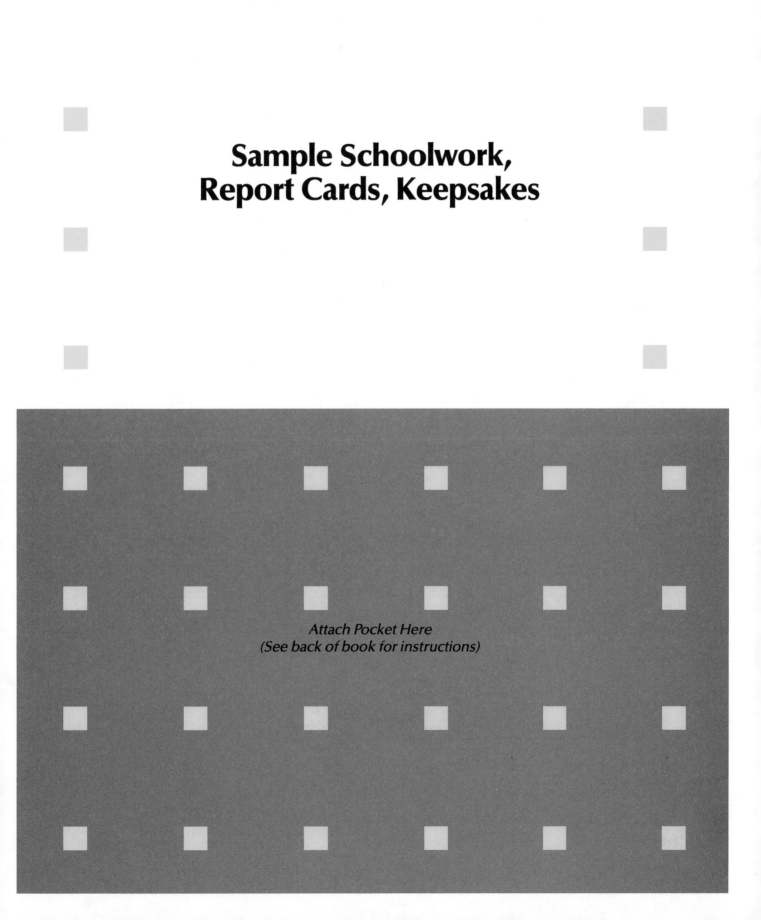

Attach Pocket Here
(See back of book for instructions)

Favorites

Friends _____

_____

_____

Books _____

_____

Music _____

_____

Sports _____

Teams _____

Television Shows _____

_____

Movies and Videos _____

_____

Clothes _____

Foods _____

_____

Places to Go _____

_____

Things to Do _____

_____

Attach Child's Photo Here

Age _____ Height _____ Weight _____

Child's Signature _____

Thoughts About My Child This Year _____

_____

_____

_____

_____

_____

GRADE 6

School _____

Address _____

Teachers _____   _____

_____   _____

_____   _____

Attach Class Photo
or Pictures of Classmates Here

Classmates

_____   _____

_____   _____

_____   _____

_____   _____

_____   _____

_____   _____

_____   _____

Most Favorite Subject _____

Least Favorite Subject _____

Favorite Teacher _____

Other Influential People _____

_____

Greatest Accomplishment This School Year _____

_____

School Activities and Projects _____

_____

_____

Special Talents _____

_____

Hobbies and Interests _____

_____

_____

Aspirations and Goals _____

_____

Highlights of the Year

Trip to _____ Date _____

Details _____

_____

Party for _____ Date _____

Details _____

_____

_____

_____

Special Event _____ Date _____

Details _____

_____

*Attach Photos
or Souvenirs Here*

Summer Activities _____

_____

_____

Sample Schoolwork,
Report Cards, Keepsakes

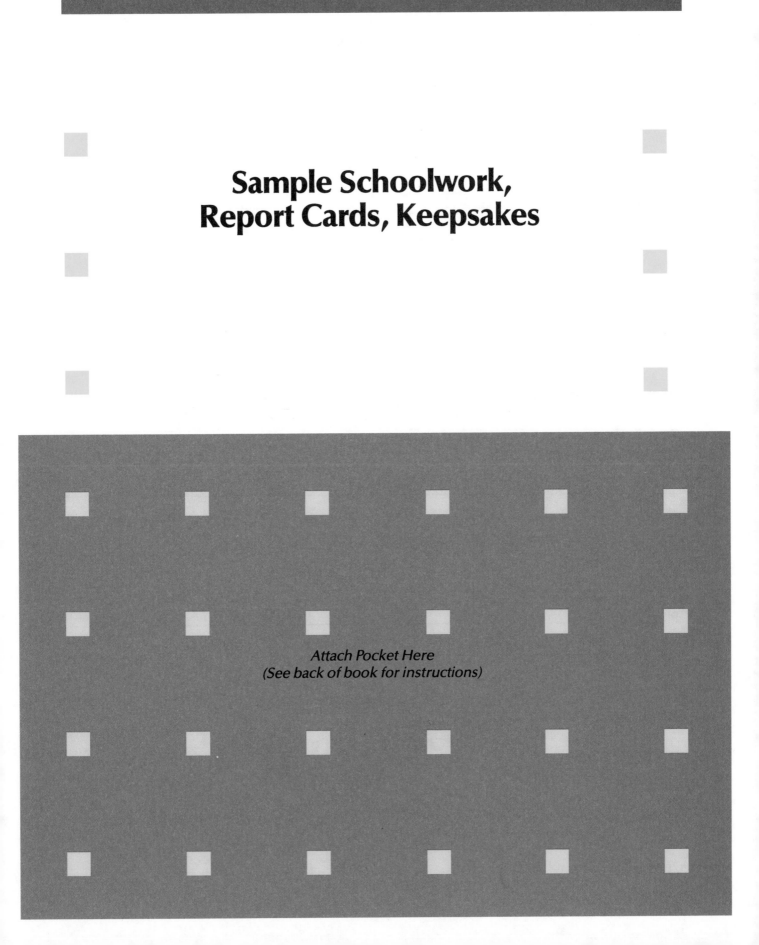

Attach Pocket Here
(See back of book for instructions)

Favorites

Friends _____

_____

_____

Books _____

_____

Music _____

_____

Sports _____

Teams _____

Television Shows _____

_____

Movies and Videos _____

_____

Clothes _____

Foods _____

_____

Places to Go _____

_____

Things to Do _____

_____

Attach Child's Photo Here

Age _____ Height _____ Weight _____

Child's Signature _____

Thoughts About My Child This Year _____

_____

_____

_____

_____

_____

GRADE 7

School _____

Address _____

Teachers

_____   _____

_____   _____

_____   _____

_____   _____

_____   _____

*Attach Photos
of Classmates Here*

Favorite Subjects _____

_____

Favorite Teachers _____

Other Influential People _____

_____

_____

Greatest Accomplishment This School Year _____

_____

_____

School Activities and Projects _____

_____

_____

Special Talents _____

_____

_____

Hobbies and Interests _____

_____

Aspirations and Goals _____

_____

_____

Highlights of the Year

Trip to _____ Date _____

Details _____

_____

Party for _____ Date _____

Details _____

_____

Sporting Event _____ Date _____

Details _____

_____

Special Event _____ Date _____

Details _____

_____

*Attach Photos
or Souvenirs Here*

Summer Activities _____

_____

_____

_____

Sample Schoolwork,
Report Cards, Keepsakes

Attach Pocket Here
(See back of book for instructions)

Favorites

Friends _____

_____

_____

Books _____

_____

Music _____

_____

Sports _____

Teams _____

Television Shows _____

Movies and Videos _____

_____

Clothes _____

Foods _____

Places to Go _____

_____

Things to Do _____

_____

_____

Attach Child's Photo Here

Age _____ Height _____ Weight _____

Child's Signature _____

Thoughts About My Child This Year _____

_____

_____

_____

_____

_____

GRADE 8

School _____

Address _____

Teachers

_____   _____

_____   _____

_____   _____

_____   _____

_____   _____

Attach Photos
of Classmates Here

Favorite Subjects _____

_____

Favorite Teachers _____

Other Influential People _____

_____

_____

Greatest Accomplishment This School Year _____

_____

_____

School Activities and Projects _____

_____

_____

Special Talents _____

_____

_____

Hobbies and Interests _____

_____

Aspirations and Goals _____

_____

_____

Highlights of the Year

Trip to _____ Date _____

Details _____

_____

Party for _____ Date _____

Details _____

_____

Sporting Event _____ Date _____

Details _____

_____

Special Event _____ Date _____

Details _____

_____

*Attach Photos
or Souvenirs Here*

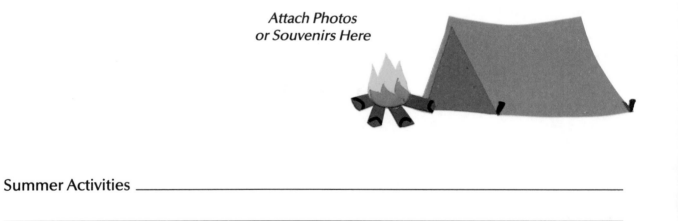

Summer Activities _____

_____

_____

_____

Sample Schoolwork,
Report Cards, Keepsakes

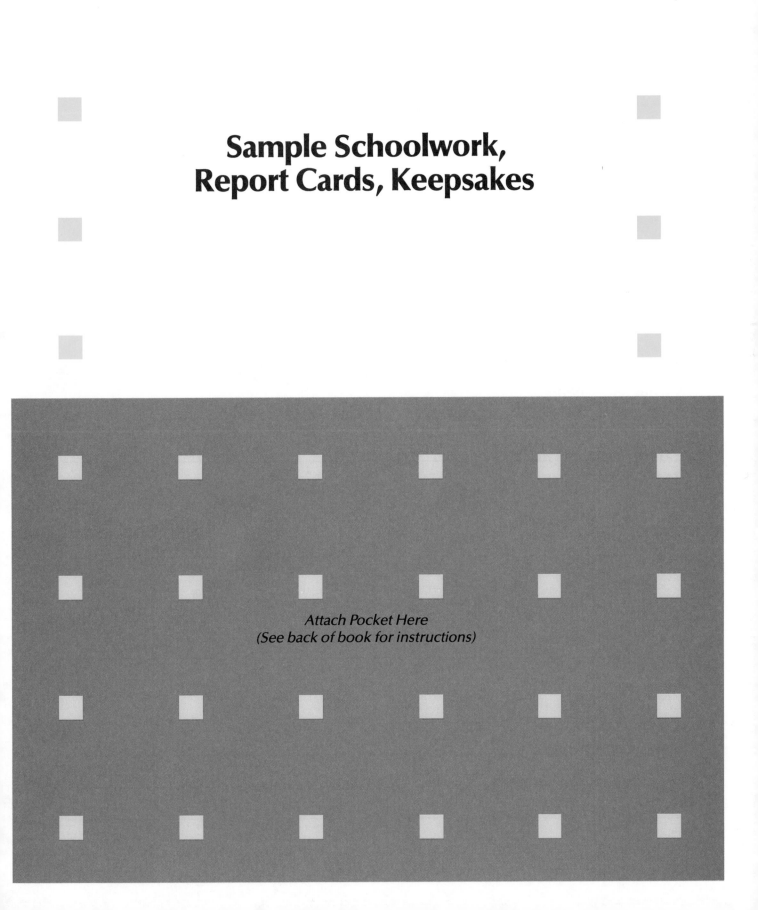

Attach Pocket Here
(See back of book for instructions)

Favorites

Friends _____

_____

_____

Books _____

_____

Music _____

_____

Sports _____

Teams _____

Television Shows _____

Movies and Videos _____

_____

Clothes _____

Foods _____

Places to Go _____

_____

Things to Do _____

_____

_____

Attach Child's Photo Here

Age _____ Height _____ Weight _____

Child's Signature _____

Thoughts About My Child This Year _____

_____

_____

_____

_____

_____

GRADE 9

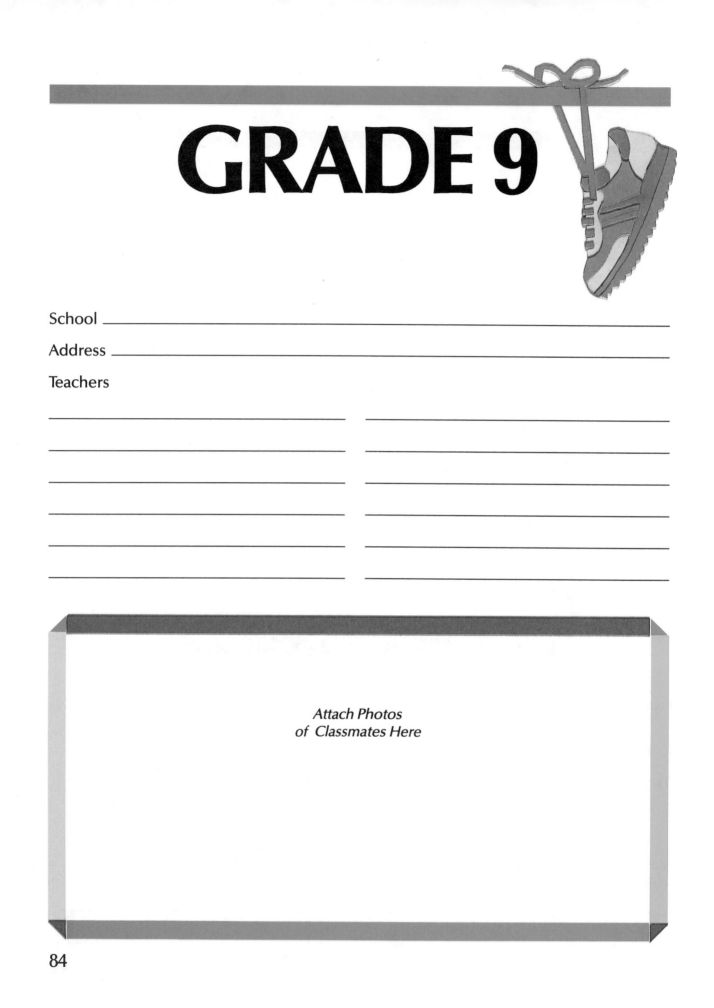

School _____

Address _____

Teachers

_____   _____

_____   _____

_____   _____

_____   _____

_____   _____

_____   _____

*Attach Photos
of Classmates Here*

Best Subjects _____

_____

Favorite Teachers _____

Other Influential People _____

_____

Greatest Accomplishment This School Year _____

_____

_____

School Activities and Projects _____

_____

_____

_____

Other Interests and Activities _____

_____

_____

_____

_____

Aspirations and Goals _____

_____

_____

_____

Highlights of the Year

Trip to _____ Date _____

Details _____

_____

Party for _____ Date _____

Details _____

_____

Sporting Event _____ Date _____

Details _____

_____

Special Event _____ Date _____

Details _____

_____

*Attach Photos
or Souvenirs Here*

Summer Activities _____

_____

_____

_____

Sample Schoolwork, Report Cards, Keepsakes

Attach Pocket Here
(See back of book for instructions)

Favorites

Friends _____

_____

_____

_____

Things to Do _____

_____

Places to Go _____

_____

Clothes _____

_____

Foods _____

Sports _____

Teams _____

Music _____

_____

Books _____

_____

Movies and Videos _____

_____

Television Shows _____

_____

Attach Photo Here

Age _____ Height _____ Weight _____

Signature _____

Thoughts About My Child This Year _____

_____

_____

_____

_____

_____

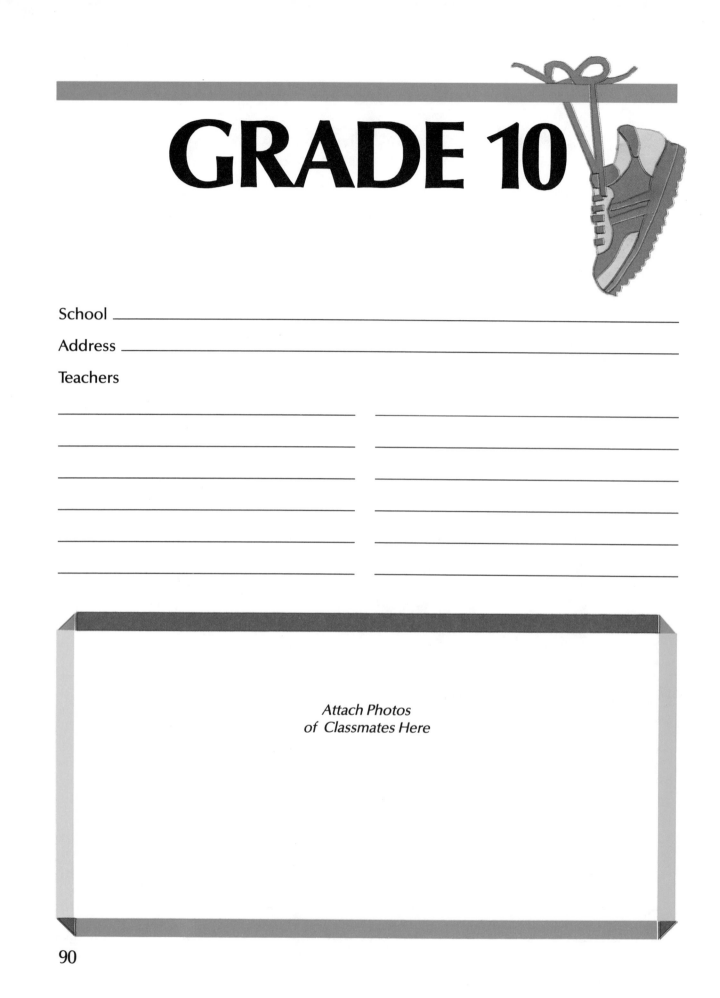

GRADE 10

School _____

Address _____

Teachers

_____   _____

_____   _____

_____   _____

_____   _____

_____   _____

_____   _____

*Attach Photos
of Classmates Here*

Best Subjects _____

Favorite Teachers _____

Other Influential People _____

Greatest Accomplishment This School Year _____

School Activities and Projects _____

Other Interests and Activities _____

Aspirations and Goals _____

Highlights of the Year

Trip to _____ Date _____

Details _____

_____

Party for _____ Date _____

Details _____

_____

Sporting Event _____ Date _____

Details _____

_____

Special Event _____ Date _____

Details _____

_____

*Attach Photos
or Souvenirs Here*

Summer Activities _____

_____

_____

_____

Sample Schoolwork, Report Cards, Keepsakes

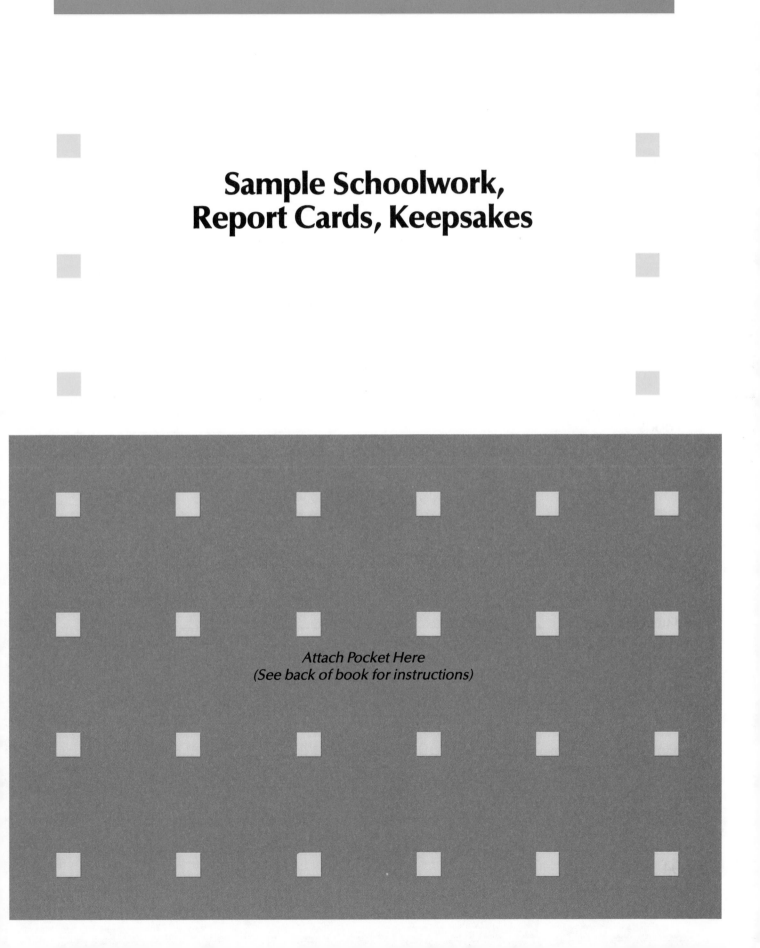

Attach Pocket Here
(See back of book for instructions)

Favorites

Friends _____

_____

_____

_____

Things to Do _____

_____

Places to Go _____

_____

Clothes _____

_____

Foods _____

Sports _____

Teams _____

Music _____

_____

Books _____

_____

Movies and Videos _____

_____

Television Shows _____

_____

Attach Photo Here

Age _____ Height _____ Weight _____

Signature _____

Thoughts About My Child This Year _____

_____

_____

_____

_____

_____

GRADE 11

School _____

Address _____

Teachers

_____   _____
_____   _____
_____   _____
_____   _____
_____   _____
_____   _____

*Attach Photos
of Classmates Here*

Outstanding Subject _____

Most Influential Teacher _____

Other Influential People _____

_____

Greatest Accomplishment This School Year _____

_____

_____

School Activities and Projects _____

_____

_____

_____

Other Interests and Activities _____

_____

_____

_____

After-School Jobs or Volunteer Work _____

_____

Aspirations and Goals_____

_____

_____

_____

Highlights of the Year

Trip to _____ Date _____

Details _____

_____

Trip to _____ Date _____

Details _____

_____

Party for _____ Date _____

Details _____

_____

Sporting Event _____ Date _____

Details _____

_____

Special Event _____ Date _____

Details _____

_____

*Attach Photos
or Souvenirs Here*

Summer Activities

_____

_____

Sample Schoolwork,
Report Cards, Keepsakes

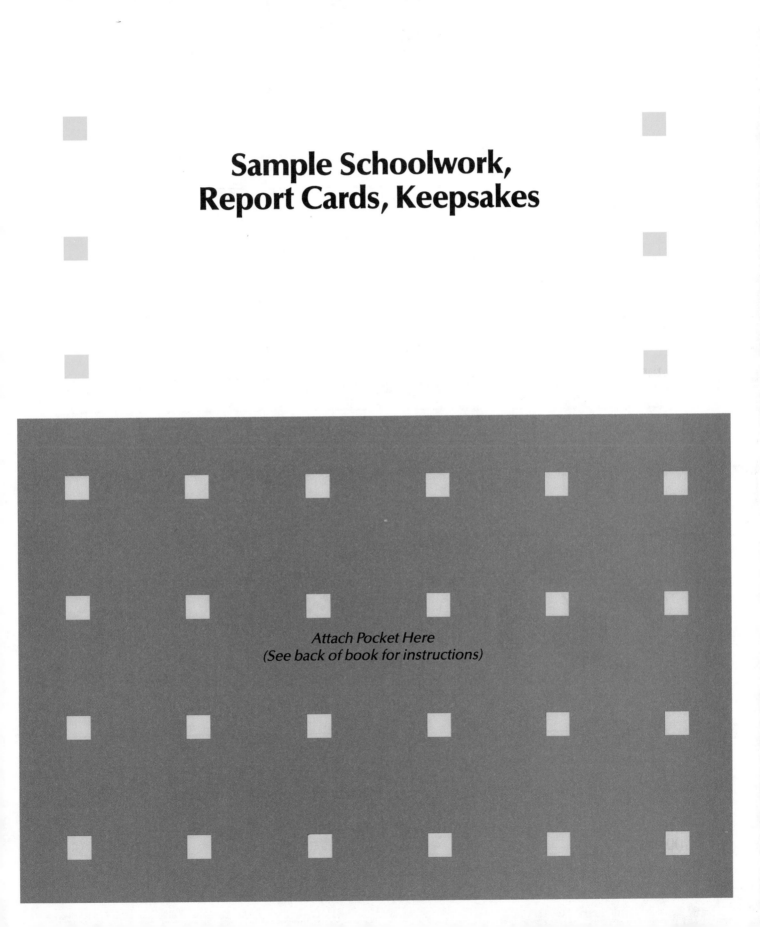

Attach Pocket Here
(See back of book for instructions)

Favorites

Friends _____

_____

_____

_____

Things to Do _____

_____

_____

Places to Go _____

_____

Clothes _____

Foods _____

Sports _____

Teams _____

Music _____

_____

Books _____

_____

Movies and Videos _____

_____

Attach Photo Here

Age _____ Height _____ Weight _____

Signature _____

Thoughts About My Child This Year _____

_____

_____

_____

_____

_____

GRADE 12

School _____

Address _____

Teachers

_____   _____

_____   _____

_____   _____

_____   _____

_____   _____

*Attach Photos
of Classmates Here*

Outstanding Subject _____

Most Influential Teacher _____

Other Influential People _____

_____

Greatest Accomplishment This School Year _____

_____

_____

School Activities and Projects _____

_____

_____

_____

Other Interests and Activities _____

_____

_____

_____

After-School Jobs or Volunteer Work _____

_____

Aspirations and Goals _____

_____

_____

_____

Highlights of the Year

Trip to _____ Date _____

Details _____

_____

Trip to _____ Date _____

Details _____

_____

Party for _____ Date _____

Details _____

_____

Sporting Event _____ Date _____

Details _____

_____

Special Event _____ Date _____

Details _____

_____

*Attach Photos
or Souvenirs Here*

Summer Activities

_____

_____

Sample Schoolwork, Report Cards, Keepsakes

Attach Pocket Here
(See back of book for instructions)

Favorites

Friends _____

_____

_____

_____

Things to Do _____

_____

_____

Places to Go _____

_____

Clothes _____

Foods _____

Sports _____

Teams _____

Music _____

_____

Books _____

_____

Movies and Videos _____

_____

Attach Photo Here

Age _____ Height _____ Weight _____

Signature _____

Thoughts About My Child This Year _____

_____

_____

_____

_____

_____

Graduation

Date _____

School _____

Location of Ceremony _____

*Attach Invitation
or Announcement Here*

Guests

_____   _____

_____   _____

_____   _____

Special Memories of the Ceremony _____

_____

_____

A Celebration at _____

Details _____

_____

A Graduation Party at _____

Details _____

_____

Gifts   From

_____   _____

_____   _____

_____   _____

_____   _____

_____   _____

Attach Photo
of the Graduate Here

Future Plans _____

_____

Medical Record

Growth

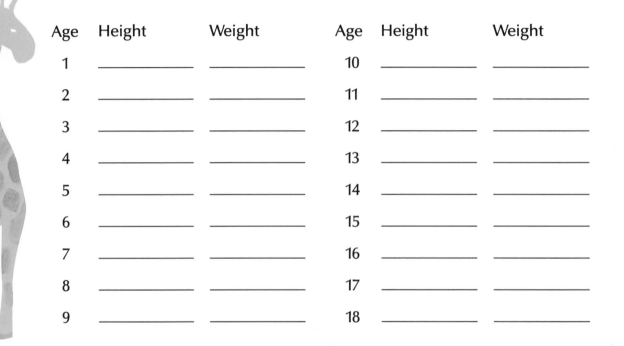

Age	Height	Weight	Age	Height	Weight
1	_____	_____	10	_____	_____
2	_____	_____	11	_____	_____
3	_____	_____	12	_____	_____
4	_____	_____	13	_____	_____
5	_____	_____	14	_____	_____
6	_____	_____	15	_____	_____
7	_____	_____	16	_____	_____
8	_____	_____	17	_____	_____
9	_____	_____	18	_____	_____

Immunizations

	Dates				
Smallpox	_____	_____	_____	_____	_____
Diphtheria, Pertussis, Tetanus	_____	_____	_____	_____	_____
Polio	_____	_____	_____	_____	_____
Measles	_____	_____	_____	_____	_____
Rubella	_____	_____	_____	_____	_____
Mumps	_____	_____	_____	_____	_____

Major Illnesses

Dates

_____ _____

_____ _____

_____ _____

_____ _____

_____ _____

_____ _____

_____ _____

_____ _____

Eye Examinations

Date _____ Results _____

Date _____ Results _____

Date _____ Results _____

Ear Examinations

Date _____ Results _____

Date _____ Results _____

Allergies

	Date Determined	Treatment
_____	_____	_____
_____	_____	_____

Hospitalizations

Date _____ Reason _____

Date _____ Reason _____

Date _____ Reason _____

Additional Medical Information _____

_____

_____

Dental Record

First Baby Tooth _____
                                date

First Tooth to Fall Out _____
                                date

First Adult Tooth _____
                                date

Examinations, X-Rays, Cleanings, Fluoride Treatments, Fillings

Date	Treatment	Date	Treatment
_____	_____	_____	_____
_____	_____	_____	_____
_____	_____	_____	_____
_____	_____	_____	_____
_____	_____	_____	_____
_____	_____	_____	_____

Braces _____

Additional Information _____

Keepsake Pockets

Throughout this album there are pages set aside for keepsake pockets, in which you can store your child's report cards, sample schoolwork, and mementos. To make each pocket, follow these simple instructions:

1. Using sharp scissors or a knife and a ruler, cut out one of the pockets on the perforated lines.

2. Turn the pocket face down and sparingly apply an adhesive such as rubber cement or glue to the areas marked "glue." (Do not use a water-based adhesive; it may wrinkle or warp the paper.)

3. Carefully place the pocket in position on the designated page and blot up any excess cement or glue.

4. Leave the album open until the adhesive is thoroughly dry.

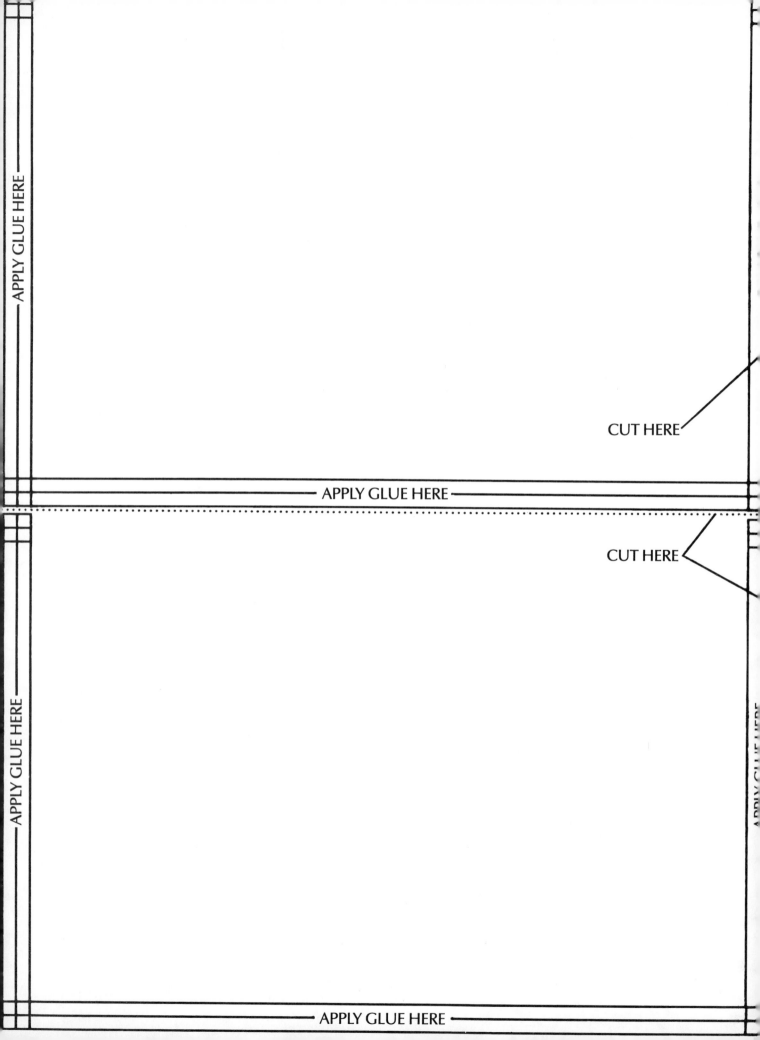

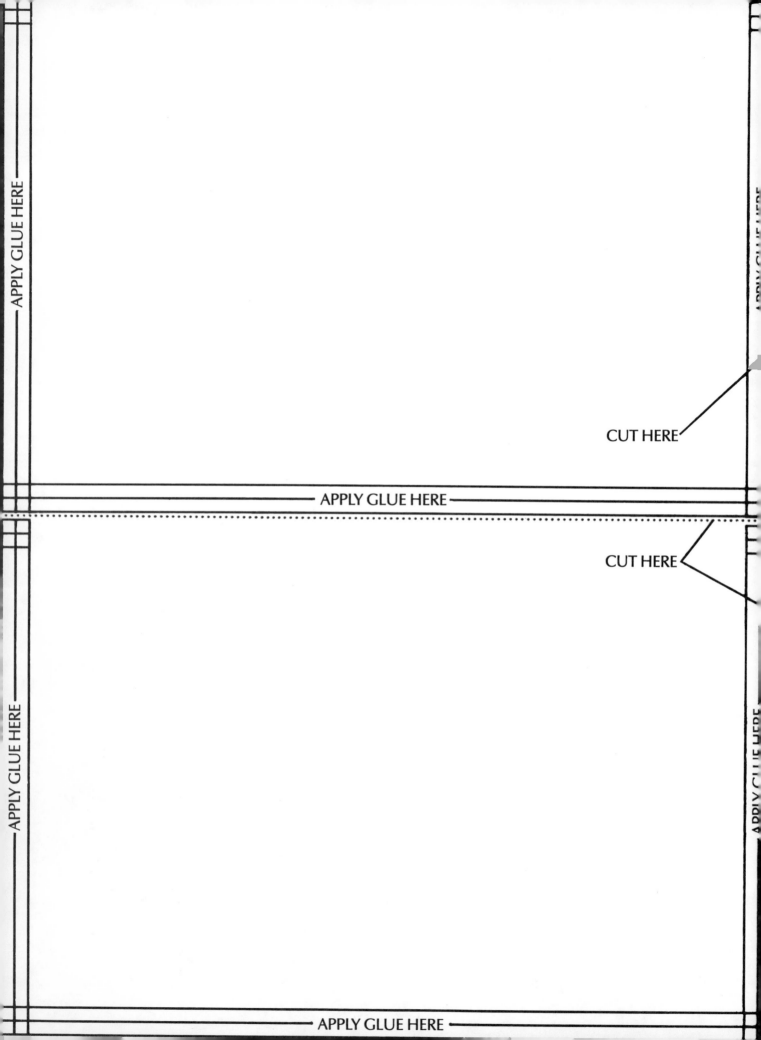

APPLY GLUE HERE

APPLY GLUE HERE

CUT HERE

APPLY GLUE HERE

CUT HERE

APPLY GLUE HERE

APPLY GLUE HERE

APPLY GLUE HERE

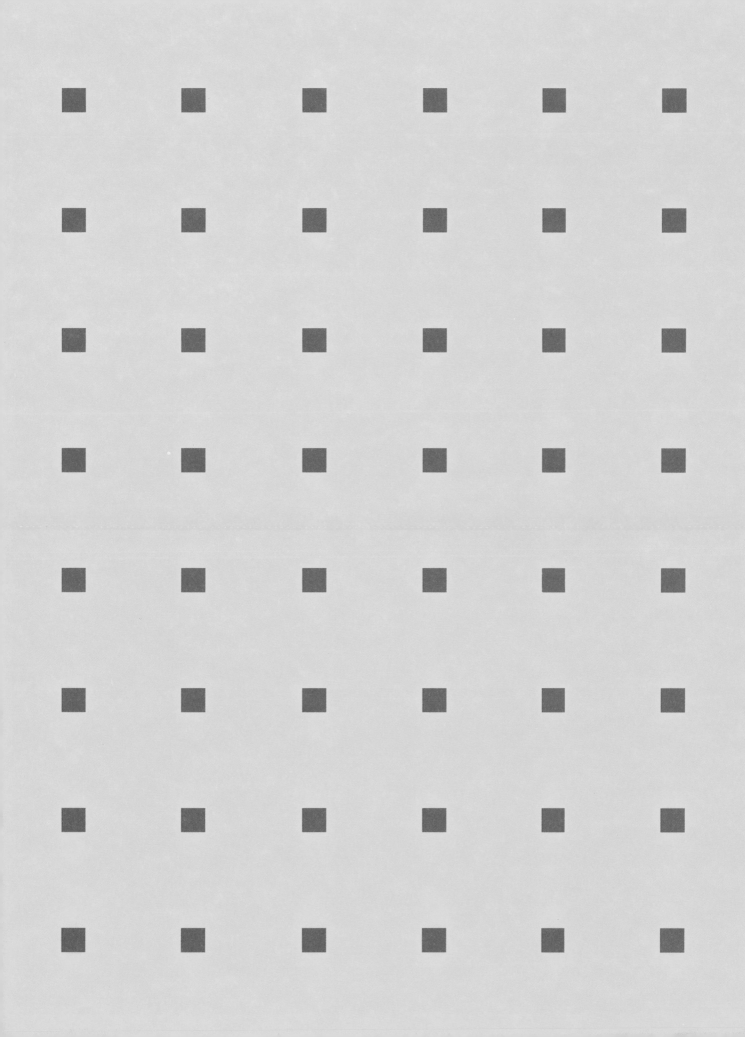

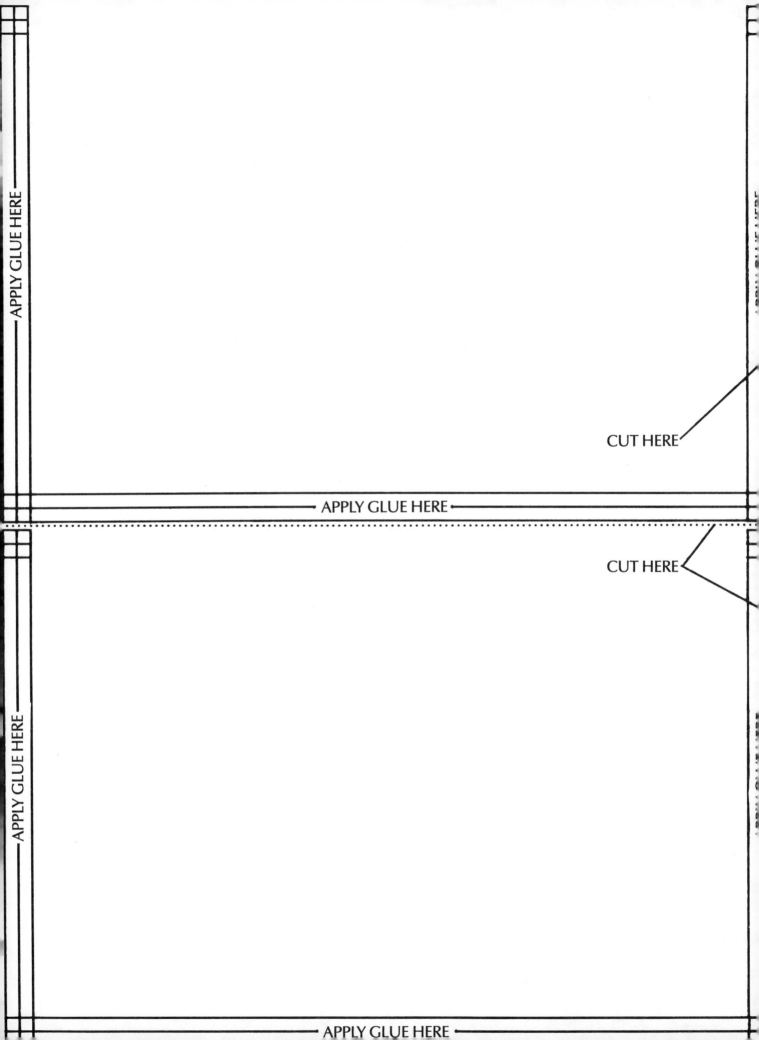

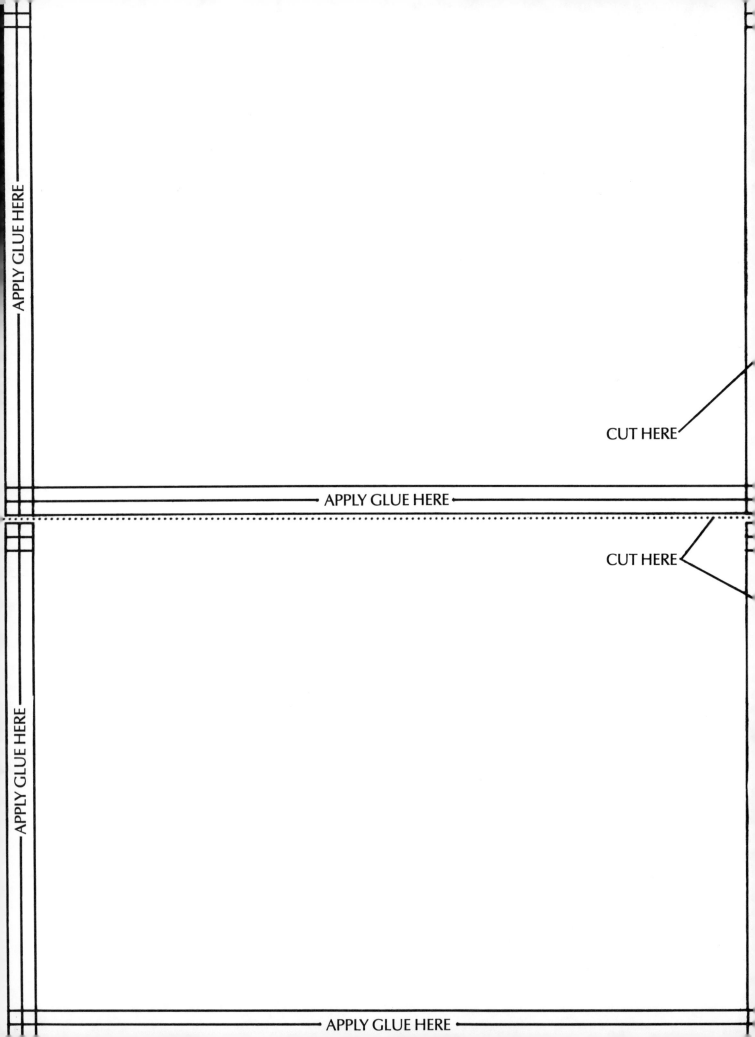

APPLY GLUE HERE

CUT HERE

APPLY GLUE HERE

CUT HERE

APPLY GLUE HERE

APPLY GLUE HERE

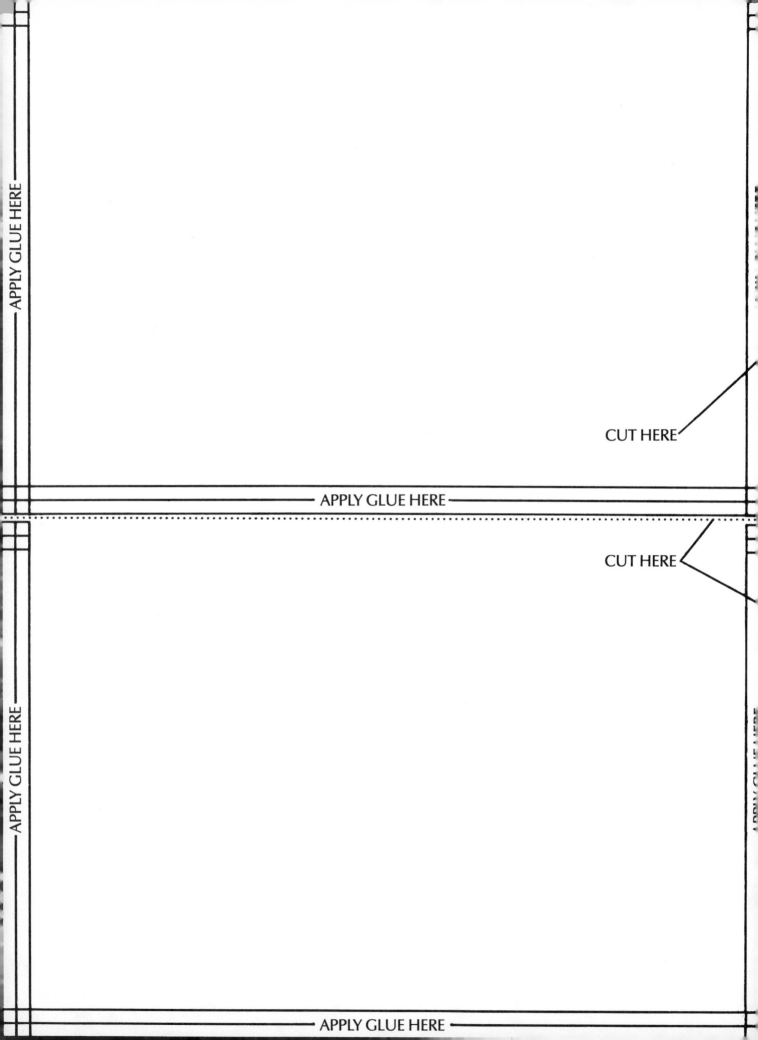

APPLY GLUE HERE

CUT HERE

APPLY GLUE HERE

CUT HERE

APPLY GLUE HERE

APPLY GLUE HERE

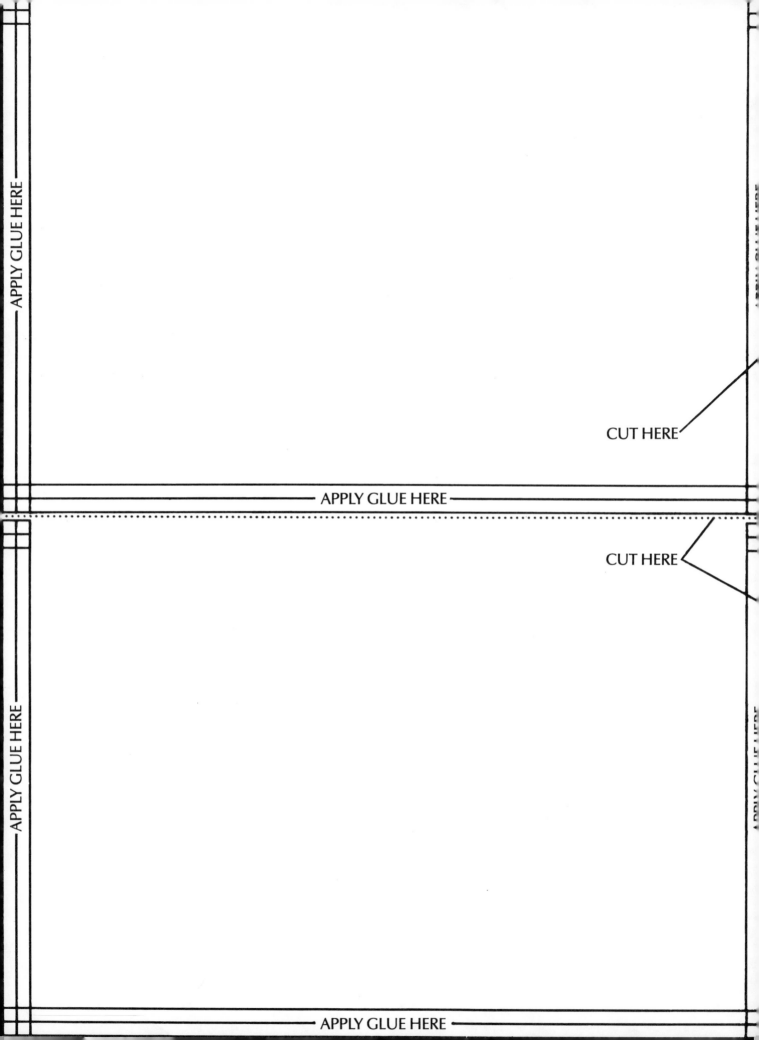

APPLY GLUE HERE

APPLY GLUE HERE

APPLY GLUE HERE

APPLY GLUE HERE

CUT HERE

CUT HERE

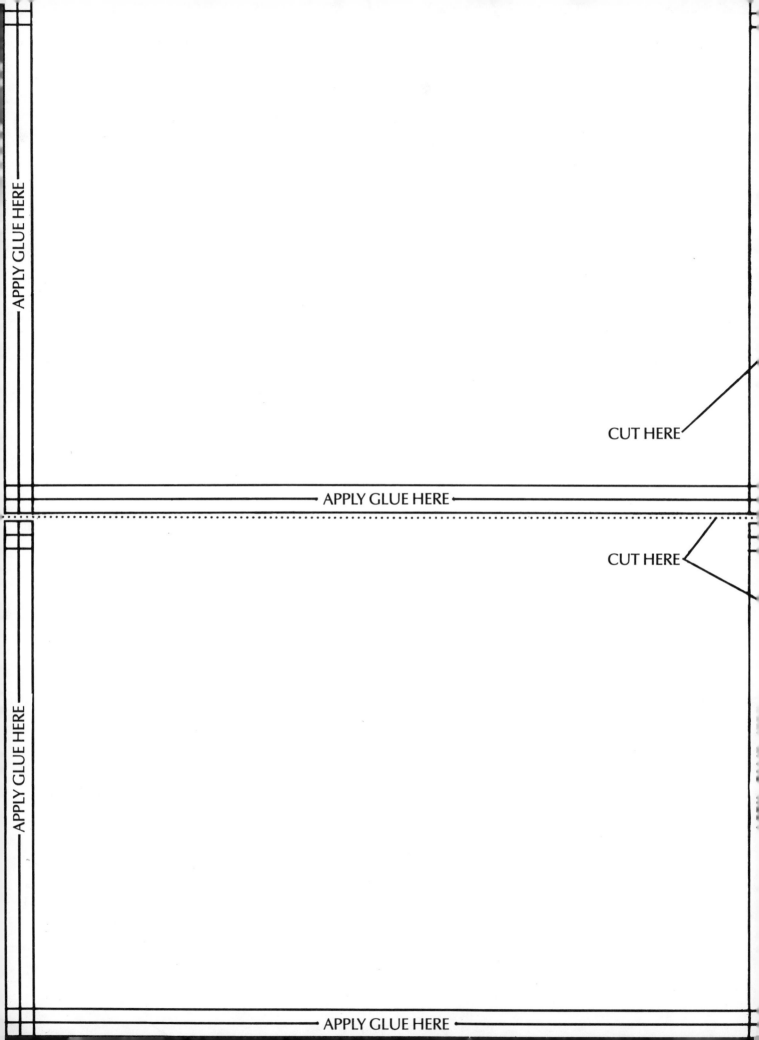

APPLY GLUE HERE

APPLY GLUE HERE

CUT HERE

APPLY GLUE HERE

CUT HERE

APPLY GLUE HERE